TENNIS
It Serves You Right!

Eric Nicol & Dave More

TENNIS

It Serves You Right!

Hurtig Publishers
Edmonton

To Mitsu

Hurtig Publishers Ltd.
10560–105 Street
Edmonton, Alberta
Canada   T5H 2W7

Canadian Cataloguing in Publication Data

Nicol, Eric, 1919–
    Tennis, it serves you right!

ISBN 0-88830-266-5

1. Tennis – Anecdotes, facetiae, satire, etc.
I. More, Dave.   II. Title.
GV996.N52 1984   796.342′02′07   C84-091285-4

Printed and bound in Canada
by T.H. Best Printing Company Ltd.

"I had as leve tosse a ball here alone as to
play at the tenys over the corde with the."

John Palgrave (d. 1554)

"Item, that no man play at tenys or pame
withyn the yeld halle."

English Gilds

"The f——ing ball was out a foot!"

Vitas Gerulaitis,
Invocation to an Umpire,
1981

Bjorn-again tennis player

Contents

Warm-up

The question is quite simple: Can you play tennis and still remain a nice person? The answer: Yes. You may even win occasionally, if your opponent has also taken the trouble to read this book.

The main thing is to avoid *serious* tennis, which can have the same effect on the personality as membership in the Nazi SS.

Other tennis books try to improve your game. That is a rotten thing to do. Lives have been ruined by such an approach, not to mention the cost of having to keep taking your white shorts to the laundromat.

The book you hold in your hands has a much more worthwhile purpose: to improve *you*, even though you play tennis regularly and sometimes feel competitive in spite of having attended a public school.

The authors have played enough tennis to know well how easily it can become a chippy contest waged by immature people. We too have been booed—all the more remarkable since no one was watching us. However, by analyzing the social effects of the game, instead of actually playing it and getting all sweaty, Nicol and More have done for tennis what Masters and Johnson did for sex, namely, shown how expertise can take the fun out of *anything*.

First, though, let us examine certain assumptions:

- the serious tennis player eliminates the gap between first and second childhood.
- he is subject to tantrums, tossing his racket, eating his balls, sometimes assuming the foetal position and refusing to come out.
- when someone tells him to get a grip on himself, he takes a handful of sawdust out of his pocket and makes a mess.

These negative ideas result from the fact that the tennis player has *a bad image*. On TV soaps, when they want to show a character as selfish, status-seeking, or morally bankrupt, they present him playing tennis. A female character wearing tennis shorts and carrying a racket identifies herself immediately as a rich tramp.

Just the way she unzips her tote bag tells us that she sleeps around, though not necessarily on the court.

The reputation of tennis as a game for spoiled brats can be blamed mostly on the behaviour of the professionals. The John McEnroes, the Jimmy Connorses, the Ilie Nastases, the Ivan Lendls have reinforced the definition of tennis as "a man's game that is played by boys." They are emotionally incontinent. The pro tennis player leaves the court in the middle of a match to have his diaper changed. Unlike the pro football or hockey player, he is not willing to play while hurt even though his mother comes out of the stands and tells him to.

The female tennis pro, while less bitchy than the male, appears to be anxious to get the match over with so that she can have a nervous breakdown. Those pros who return to tennis after motherhood are suspected of eating their young.

For both sexes, the standard of minimum physical contact in human relations is set by two pros shaking hands after a match.

Camaraderie we do not associate with tennis. TV beer commercials rarely show us a roistering group of tennis players jovially bunched around bottles of light. Nobody knows for sure what professional tennis players drink, but they probably have trouble with the nipple.

Some tennis therapists (not us) believe that the game can be made less mean-spirited by changing it into more of a contact sport, the player being encouraged to leap over the net to flatten his opponent, knock his teeth out, break his leg, or engage in any of the other acts of physical violence that bind drinking buddies together. The authors are against this because it is so hard to get both grass stains *and* blood out of a white shirt.

How, then, *do* you avoid becoming a tennis pro? Or, worse, a serious tennis player who never gets past the first round of the club tournament?

This may not be easy. If you have a natural aptitude for the game, and your parents catch you beating the pants off some other kid, you may be in trouble. The symptoms of serious tennis are insidious: putting on shoes to play . . . practising, against a backboard . . . having your whole racket restrung when only one string is broken.

Don't let this happen to you.

In the chapters that follow, the authors explain why a tennis player becomes the sort of person you wouldn't want to go fishing with. If you wish to remain your old, lovable self (and who doesn't?), do *not* follow any of the lessons described in these pages. Remember that serious tennis is highly infectious. The happy-go-lucky Australian greats—Newcombe, Rosewall, Laver—succeeded in remaining affable, beer-drinking, congenial guys only because Australia is an isolated continent, favouring unusual forms of life. You probably lack the environmental advantages of the wombat.

Even the Down-Under pros of today appear to have succumbed to sourpuss tennis.

For you, too, it may already be later than you think. When was the last time you shouted "Jolly good shot!" to your opponent rather than yourself? Have you separated from your wife, or husband, because that spouse kept having a fit of the giggles on the tennis court?

Take heart. It is never too late for the tennis player to reconstitute himself as a human being. Sainthood may be a visionary goal, for him or her playing this fascinating but personality-distorting game. But there is no need to remain an emotional cripple merely because one doesn't find many tennis rackets among the crutches cast away at Lourdes.

In order to play tennis and remain a Pleasant Person, however, you must be familiar with the basically snotty history of the game. As follows.

EN & DM

Court Tennis

"...my high-blown pride
At length broke under me, and now
has left me,
Weary and old with service ..."

(*Henry VIII*, Act III, Sc. 2, l. 352)

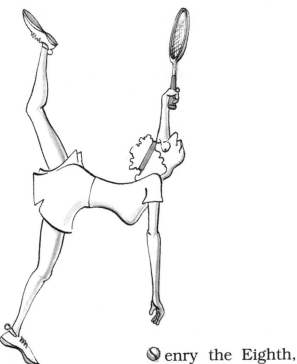

 enry the Eighth, Britain's least lovable monarch, played tennis. His indoor tennis court is still playable at Hampton Court, where Henry defined the winner of a set as the first to take six wives.

He is also credited with having supplemented the forehand chop and the backhand chop with the both-hands chop. Historians disagree on whether the fact that Henry the Eighth played tennis had anything to do with his fierce argument with the Holy Roman Umpire, which in turn led to his being excommunicated and barred from the Italian Open.

There is no doubt, however, that the robust English monarch used his tennis court regularly to warm up before going to war with Scotland. Instead of building a tennis court of their own, the stubborn Scots remained Catholic, as well as playing golf which weakened their belief in God.

The tennis that Henry the Eighth played on his private court is called, somewhat predictably, *court tennis*. Also known as tennis royal, court tennis is believed to have originated in medieval France, about

1. New balls

the fourteenth century, with a French knight seeking an alternative to The Hundred Years' War.

As the first step towards making the contest safer, the French knight got off his horse. According to one theory about the invention of tennis, two French chevaliers who had jousted each other off their mounts tried to continue the duel by batting horse apples at one another. This story is probably apocryphal, since the heavy armour of the time would have made it difficult to apply topspin.

2. New Anne

Mosaic tennis

What is historical fact is that tennis quickly became very popular in France, though the nobles had to play the game indoors so that the starving peasants would not see them unmounted and get dangerous ideas about their being common mortals. (Today, the French horse has been replaced by the Peugeot, but the private tennis club still screens out commoners lest they see that the mighty have courts of clay.)

The francogenesis of tennis is shown in the name of the game (tennis), which is derived from the Old French, probably from the word *tenez* ("take") as in

"Take this!" spoken by the player before slamming the ball at his opponent. The derivation is certainly in keeping with the spirit of the game, which helped to train French artillery officers how to duck. (Hence the theory that Napoleon was pictured reaching into his vest for the second ball.)

The same snarky tone marks the origin of the word *love* as used in tennis. Tennis gave the world the only love game without bodily contact. In tennis, love has nothing to do with affection. *Au contraire*. As every schoolboy knows, *love* comes from the French word *l'oeuf*, or egg. The player shouting "l'oeuf!" derisively at an opponent was rubbing it in that his adversary was sitting on a goose fruit. (Cricketers say a batsman has "broken his duck," but there is less egg on his face.)

The tennis player also owes to the French the word *deuce*, used when the score is tied at 40. It is popularly believed that *deuce* is a mild form of *devil*, as in "Deuce take you, unclean person!" A reasonable assumption, given the ill temper of tennis. More likely, however, is that *deuce* comes from *deux*, meaning that the server must gain two more consecutive points in order to win the game. From the advantage score the game can revert to deuce any number of times, making tennis one of the few games that go backwards. With enough returns to deuce the player may be made to feel that his whole life has been a regression. He may show signs of reverting to infantilism: sucking the thumb, playing with the genitals, etc. Hence the excessive whining

23

associated with protracted games of tennis, as well as geophagia or dirt eating, a lamentable childishness that can gradually erode the entire playing surface of the court.

Deuce typifies the deliberately complicated scoring of court tennis, devised by the French to make it easier to cheat. Tennis players sometimes wonder why the scoring should be 15, 30, 40, advantage, and game.

Prototype volley

Why not 1, 2, 3, 4, and Bob's your uncle? Answer: Too simple. The ability to count higher than 10 (*i.e.*, without using the fingers) was a sign of the French upper class. Thanks to our contemporary methods of teaching mathematics, tennis scoring still creates problems for anyone whose calculator batteries have worn out and makes it more difficult to win an athletic scholarship.

To help them keep the complex score of court tennis the players use marks on the floor. Indeed the whole building is specifically constructed to satisfy the player who has the soul of an income-tax accountant. It is described by the *Century Dictionary and Encyclopedia* as follows:

> The court (96 feet by 32) is surrounded by a wall, from which a sloping roof called the *penthouse* extends on three sides to an interior wall 7 feet high; and a net 5 feet high at the ends to 3 feet in the middle is placed across the court. The first player (the *server*) hits the ball with a racket so that it strikes the penthouse or the wall above it, and rebounds into the court on his opponent's side of the net. The opposing player (the *striker-out*) has to strike the ball back into the server's court before it strikes the ground or on its first bound. The player who is the first to drive the ball into the net or beyond the prescribed boundary loses a stroke. If a player fails to return the ball before it strikes the ground twice, a *chase* is noted against him on the marked floor. This does not count at the time, but a stroke may be won or lost from it by subsequent play. When two chases have been made, or when the score of one side reaches 40, the players change ends. Strokes are won or lost in various other ways

besides those mentioned above (as by driving the ball into certain openings in the inner wall) . . .

Any game that starts with the server hitting the ball at the penthouse is obviously Snob City.

As for driving the ball into certain openings in the inner wall, our impression is strengthened that court tennis from the beginning combined the devious assault of squash with some of the practices of Renais-

Civilized tennis

sance politics. When a French noble got really good at tennis, he was ready to take a shot at murdering his younger brother. Even the service was underhand.

The Oath of the Tennis Court

Court tennis remained very popular with French royalty till the eighteenth century, when play was interrupted by the French Revolution. The aristocrats found it difficult to continue rallying because of a precipitation called the guillotine.

One of the most dramatic episodes leading up to

The rise of French tennis

the beheading of Louis XVI (which took the edge off his game) was the Oath of the Tennis Court. Some people today, influenced by the rough language they hear at the U.S. Indoor Championship, assume that the Oath of the Tennis Court was "Sacré bleu!"—accompanied by the player's biting his thumb at the royal box. Not so. The Oath occurred in Le Jeu de Paume, the king's private tennis court, when the Three Estates (clergy, nobility and commons) met there in defiance of the monarch and swore to stick together till they had a constitution and clean sneakers.

They may also have had a quick game of round-robin doubles, but this is considered unlikely since the clergy had come without their gym strip.

Le Jeu de Paume still stands today, in the Tuileries Gardens, though anyone who tries to play tennis in it will find that it is being used as a modern-art museum, and the paintings can wreck his timing.

What is more meaningful for the tennis player of our time, however, is that the Oath of the Tennis Court *made tennis a historical part of the democratization of the western world.* The old Jeu de Paume takes its place beside the meadow of Runnymede, where King John signed the Magna Carta because he was feeling the heat. It is a pity that King Louis could not similarly be persuaded to join in the birth of France's National Assembly, perhaps knocking a couple of balls around to show that he was being a good sport about the defeat of the absolute monarchy.

Evolution of tennis

(1)

(2)

(3)

(4)

Lawn Tennis

hat moved tennis outdoors? The most likely explanation is that after the French and American revolutions many more people were playing court tennis and nobody had invented the shower.

For a while the French combated the problem by developing perfumes of increasing strength, but there came a point where even shallow breathing could not contend with the atmosphere. Played on the lawn, however, with a favouring wind, tennis was quite tolerable. It remained a patrician pastime because only the titled or the nouveau riche could afford to devote a sizable rectangle of ground to an activity more frivolous than growing potatoes. Even today a privately owned lawn tennis court is a status symbol affordable mostly by Mafia godfathers, who offer the court to guests who don't know that the game is up.

Because the ball often carried into the shrubbery, lawn tennis quickly led to mixed doubles. Eventually some spoilsport thought of enclosing the court with a fence, but for a time, namely England's Victorian era, lawn tennis was a genteel version of a romp in the hay. The game underwent a temporary crisis when a lady was suspected of perspiring. Horses sweat, gentlemen perspire, and ladies are flushed: so went the semantics of porous emission. By the end of the nineteenth century the ladies playing tennis were flushing so copiously that it was necessary for them to remove one layer of petticoats. As this had no perceptible effect on the expansion of the British Empire, they also shed their bustles. Thus tennis played a significant role in the emancipation of the upper-class female from voluminous garments. A lady felt that it was preferable to risk arousing the gentlemen by exposing an ankle rather than to trip over her crinoline and suffer a fall that had no redeeming features.

Lawn tennis took another step towards being a popular, rather than a stately, pastime when the game became spirited enough to entertain people who were merely watching. Someone noticed that while bystanders dozed during cricket matches they often actu-

Australian serve

ally stayed awake beside the tennis court. Once they had overcome the dizziness caused by moving the head from side to side ("tennis neck"), they were sometimes moved to applaud the more energetic and skilful shots. Vocal appreciation, such as cheers, was severely frowned on till recent times, and therefore lawn tennis was particularly suited to the British gentry, always looking for an excuse to exercise restraint. Tennis also provided an alternative to fox hunting, for people who couldn't stand the sight of blood, especially their own blood.

In 1877, the first lawn tennis championship match was held at Wimbledon. This consecrated the sod that has remained the world's most esteemed grass grown outside Colombia.

The Clay Court

Because lawn tennis courts have a tendency to go bald at an early age, someone charged with the upkeep of a lawn court said the hell with it and called it a clay court. The big advantage of the clay court was that it did not need to be mowed. Unless, of course, it was not looked after, in which case it again became a lawn court. Some tennis courts are constantly in transition, from lawn to clay and back to lawn. The tennis player who owns such a court may be even more emotionally unstable than players who know what kind of surface they are playing on.

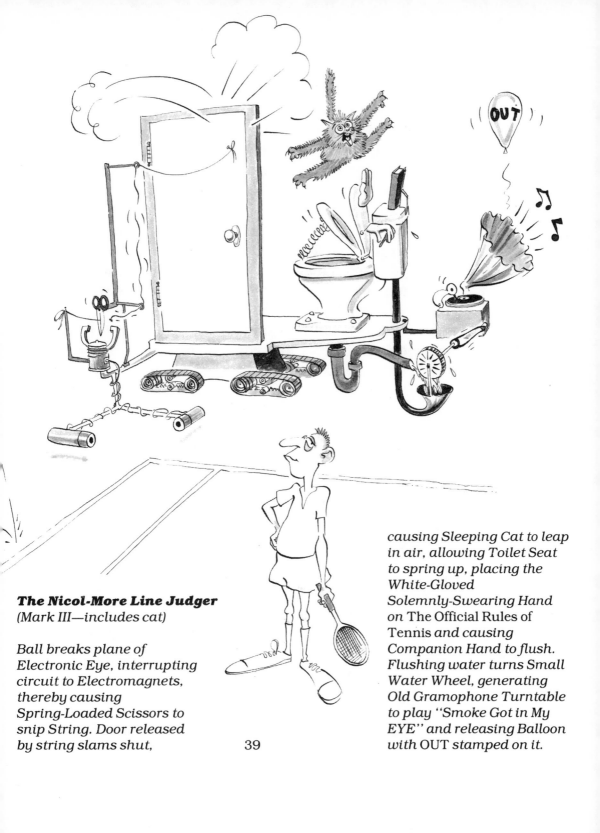

The Nicol-More Line Judger
(Mark III—includes cat)

Ball breaks plane of Electronic Eye, interrupting circuit to Electromagnets, thereby causing Spring-Loaded Scissors to snip String. Door released by string slams shut, causing Sleeping Cat to leap in air, allowing Toilet Seat to spring up, placing the White-Gloved Solemnly-Swearing Hand on The Official Rules of Tennis and causing Companion Hand to flush. Flushing water turns Small Water Wheel, generating Old Gramophone Turntable to play "Smoke Got in My EYE" and releasing Balloon with OUT stamped on it.

The clay court made a major contribution to the bitchiness of tennis because a player can protest a line call by pointing to the place that the ball scuffed in landing. Grass remains popular, however, as the player having a fit of temper finds the clay court less hospitable to bang the head on.

A variation of the clay court is the *en-tout-cas* court, which enables the tennis player to be objectionable regardless of the weather. Most public courts today have an all-weather surface that resembles a stretch of highway, complete with a line down the middle. This court attracts people who are not allowed to drive a car, for psychotic reasons, and who find release by driving a tennis ball down an alley.

Tennis in a Tent

In a partial return to the court tennis of Henry the Eighth, many clubs provide indoor courts shielded from the weather by an inflated dome. This can cause a temporary change of personality known to psychiatrists as "bubble trouble." The player accustomed to playing tennis outdoors becomes disoriented, unable to find the alibis that are an essential part of his game. Sun in the eyes, gusty winds that change ends with the victim, attack by wasp—all these natural hazards are denied to the indoor player. He can blame only himself for unforced errors, unless he can show his opponent some proof of having had an unhappy childhood: photos of the orphanage, scars from sexual abuse, etc.

The bubble also makes it harder for the player to gaze skyward, exclaiming "I say, isn't that a rare trumpeter swan?"—then serving quickly while the opponent is looking up.

Again, some tennis players depend on the very high lob, so high that the opposing player loses track of it unless he has radio contact with mission control in Houston. This lob is denied by the dome, which has the

Night tennis

psychological effect of making the player think low. He may deny God altogether. If immature, he may see the bubble as a return to the womb and play the entire match labouring under a misconception.

(*Note*: For professional tournaments the indoor court is always surrounded with floral offerings, an attempt to remind the players that they are part of nature. It never works.)

Night Tennis

More and more outdoor courts are being illuminated at night to accommodate players who are allergic to sunlight. Some of these players have rather prominent eyeteeth and learned to play the game in Transylvania. It is a mistake to assume that their mobility will be impeded by their wearing a black cape. Their style of play is to go for the jugular. Literally. They can, however, be foiled by hiding the ball, when you are serving, and substituting a garlic bulb.

Aside from having to sleep all day in a coffin, the main problem with nocturnal tennis is the bugs. It is not true that a mosquito would sooner starve to death than settle on a tennis player. Sucking blood from a tennis player, particularly a pro, may render the female mosquito sterile. But the bite itches all the same.

Snob Garb

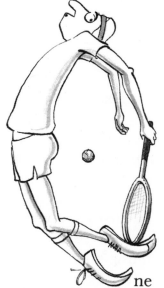

ne reason for the popularity of tennis has been that it provided upper-class people with an excuse to wear white without having to be a virgin.

In the early days of lawn tennis the ladies wore long white gowns, the gentlemen white flannel trousers, and running after the ball was considered to be vulgar. It is not recorded when the first player adopted white shorts, but the apparel won the imprimatur of the bibulous Duke of Badminton when he staggered onto the court having forgotten to put on his pants. Rather than cause him embarrassment, all the other gentlemen removed their trousers, and the ladies took off their skirts, and the pace of the game picked up immediately.

Although the tennis costume has shrunk in volume, even today many clubs require their players to wear white. This reinforces the snob appeal of tennis. A golfer can wear pink trousers and a purple shirt, without being ostracized. But the serious tennis player is expected to turn out in sparkling whites. A woman can look at a tennis player's shorts and tell at once whether he is doing his own laundry. His temper doesn't matter, but he must be able to control his bleach. As for homemade clothes, many a promising young tennis player's career has been hung up on a tennis shirt whose sleeves won't let him lower his arms below the shoulder.

As a sign of *autre temps, autres moeurs*, in the 1983 Wimbledon championship an American player, Trey Waitke, shocked the officials by turning up for his match wearing long white flannel pants and a long-sleeved white shirt with a V-neck. The tournament referee judged this to be a deliberate affront to the memory of Bill Tilden and other players of the 1930s, ordering the offender to "come with a conventional kit"—short-sleeved shirt and shorts.

This ruling effectively eliminated tennis as a refuge for the athlete with excessively knobby knees or unsightly elbows.

The same tradition requires the female tennis player to wear a short skirt over underpants whose

Victorian elegance

colour and style have been subject to American influence. When an American player named Gussie Moran appeared at Wimbledon wearing ruffle-laced panties, several of the ball boys reached puberty in her first match.

Women tennis players also wear shorter socks than men. They do this to minimize the disgrace of their socks falling down. At Wimbledon, if a player has to pull up his socks, other than figuratively, the royal

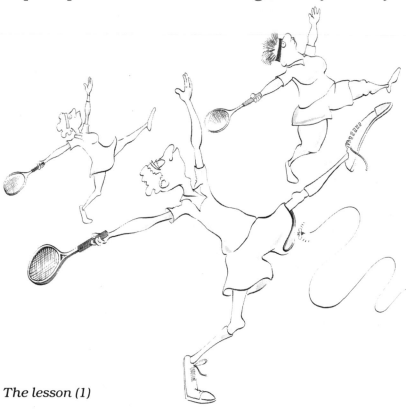

The lesson (1)

box empties at once. Male pros wear a mid-length sock that stays up out of sheer arrogance. The exception, in recent times, has been Bjorn Borg, who showed his background of Swedish socialism by wearing what appeared to be ordinary ankle-length blue-cotton socks. If the socks matched, he was having a good day. How big a factor his socks problem was in Borg's early retirement from professional tennis, no one knows. He refuses to talk about it. It does seem likely, however,

The lesson (2)

that he was never at ease facing the more aggressive hosiery of players like Jimmy Connors and John McEnroe.

Borg also often played in what looked like old sneakers. But part of the homeopathic magic of tennis as a snob sport is to wear tennis shoes that have been endorsed by a top player. One of the authors of this book has for several years bought pricey Stan Smith shoes, in the expectation that they will make him taller.

The lesson (3)

The investment failed. The author remained well under six feet, as well as pudgy around the middle. He is therefore switching to Australian Rod Laver tennis shoes. Laver shoes, unless tightly laced, will walk the player towards the nearest pub. They also give him an excuse for being somewhat bow-legged.

This trendy element in tennis is even more apparent in the choice of the most important factor in the player's becoming insufferable:

The lesson (4)

The Racquet (Racket)

A common means of intimidating an opponent, especially in a friendly game at the public park, is to walk onto the court carrying a tote bag from which project six racket handles. The authors used to do this regularly, till someone discovered that five of the handles had no heads.

The word *racket*, or *racquet*, derives like other toney tennis terms from the French: *raquette*, which in turn comes from the Arabic *rāhah*, meaning palm of the hand. It is safe to assume that tennis was originally a game of handball that developed delusions of grandeur. One conjectures that an Arab prince visited the palace of Versailles and showed the courtiers that they could reduce swelling of the palm by hitting the ball with a snowshoe. How the Arabs came to be using a snowshoe for this purpose is something of a mystery, though the last ice age may have forced some primitive handball players as far south as the present Syrian desert.

Another possibility is that the Bedouin, shepherding their sheep on nomadic treks, were able to find a market for every part of the animal except the gut. One of them, fooling around with his sheep's entrails because it was a dull night on television, wove the dried gut onto a wooden frame and—presto!—he had invented a Polish banjo. Because the strings produced only one note, however, he used the instrument to swat

flies. Thus was born the missing link between the palm of the baboon's hand and today's highly evolved Yonex R-10 ($164.95, unstrung), which is affordable mostly by Arabs who have put their sheep into oil.

In modern times the elitism of tennis has alternated between owning a steel-frame racket and one constructed of laminated wood. The Australians have always used wooden rackets. Australian tennis players are the descendants of convicts deported from Britain to Down Under. They have a natural aversion to a material that reminds them of jail-cell bars. Lately, however, the wooden frame has regained favour among players with no racial memory of leg irons.

Somewhat more specialized in appeal is the rubber-frame racket. The main advantage of the Julius Schmid "Contender" rubber racket is that it not only is more pliable but provides protection against unwanted pregnancy.

How tightly should a tennis racket be strung? As a general guideline, the more highly-strung the player, the more loosely-strung his racket. The combination of an up-tight racket and a very tense wielder can cause the head to disintegrate, and may also damage the racket. Bjorn Borg was celebrated for having his racket strung as tight as a board, but he was Swedish. Swedes can stand more tension, because of their generous pension plan.

On the other hand, if you are comfortable only if your racket is *very* loosely strung, you are probably

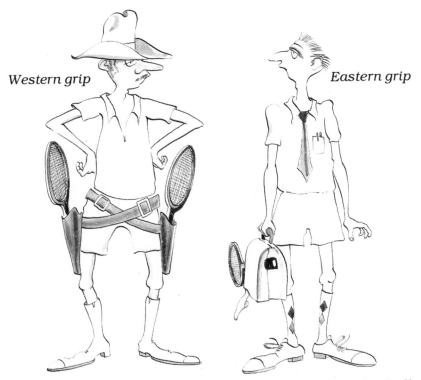

Western grip *Eastern grip*

playing lacrosse. Another clue is your putting the ball into the net instead of over it. Lacrosse is a very rough game with no social status whatever. If you play lacrosse, the authors must ask you to stop reading this book at once, before you cheapen our act.

A final note about the racket as an extension of the tennis personality: some manufacturers advertise rackets with (to quote one) "the sweetest spot on any racquet." The sweet spot is the part of the racket which, when it strikes the ball, goes "spot!" (sweetly), rather than "punk" or "fink". While the authors have never actually contacted a tennis ball with the sweet spot, we understand that to do so reduces the vibration of a mishit, which can aggravate one's dandruff problem.

More important, in our view, is that the *player* should have a sweet spot. (Not to be confused with the G-spot, which may be sweet but is restricted to mixed doubles.) All too often one observes the pro player, his face having turned litmus pink for acid, punishing his racket for not being sweet enough—throwing it, kicking it, putting sugar on it and eating it.

The tennis player should love his racket for its whole self, not just the part that feels good. Only then is he ready for marriage.

The Balls

One of the few courteous gestures in tennis is a player's holding up a clutch of woolly spheres to indicate to his opponent that he is serving with new balls. Even this formality is frequently abused by tournament pros who squeeze the two balls while staring menacingly at their opponent's crotch.

Should you make this display in a friendly game? Only if you are really desperate to remind your opponent that they are your balls that he is going to be wearing out. Against a player who uses a lot of spin shots (thereby rapidly denuding your Dunlops), this may be interpreted as a psychological weapon. In fact the whole courting rite of whose balls will be played with is peculiar to tennis. Some players, faced with

Tennis Mexicano

their opening a new container of balls, can be extremely canny (the pun is unavoidable). They bring the same unopened can to the court year after year, their finger sometimes actually in the lid ring before they accede to their opponent's saying "Let's use mine."

This is not nice. The proper player does not take advantage of the fact that in tennis, unlike ice hockey or nuclear war, the missile wears out before the player does. He rises to meet the crisis of conscience. The authors, both of whom claim Scottish ancestry, have solved the dilemma by insisting that their balls be used in the game, then producing from an old hair net a mixture of balding ovoids, in various colours, and say-

ing "I prefer to play with a lighter ball, don't you?" After rallying for a few minutes with old balls that even a moderate updraft of air launches into planetary orbit, their opponent inevitably pleads with them to let him open his new can of balls. The correct response to this request is *not* a grudging compliance, with mutters about loaded dice. Be gracious about playing with someone else's balls. Although you flub the lob, you cut down the overhead.

Magic Charms

Before leaving the subject of tennis equipment we must question the wearing of charms. It is increasingly common for players of both sexes to wear gold necklaces that they believe to have powers of a fetish, to ward off evil strokes. It is a mistake to depend too much on the magic properties of such amulets. The authors have thoroughly tested the supernatural, as a way of winning a set, one of them going so far as to convert temporarily to Catholicism, in case the cross pendant could turn his game around.

We are reluctantly forced to admit the ineffectiveness of not only the necklace but also a headband of braided monkey hair, rings whose stones have been found in chicken gizzards, and a hyena bone piercing the nose. None of these noticeably altered the dismal result, though the headband did seem to facilitate childbirth.

What does work for the benefit of professionals is the logo of commercial endorsement, as displayed on shirt, racket, shoes, or wherever there is advertising space on the body. The trend towards the tennis pro as walking billboard is not recommended for the average player, even though he has managed to become No. 10 seed in his local public courts tournament. If the amateur wishes to display his or her phone number on his shirt, as a public service, that is a matter of taste. But other endorsements, such as EAT AT DUFFY'S across the seat of the pants, detract from the simple dignity of your game.

Court Etiquette

olite tennis begins well before the start of actual play. That is, the player goes to the court, whether public or private, either (a) in the company of the person he intends to play against, or (b) in the hope of picking up an opponent while waiting on the bench. To deal with (b) first:

The tennis pick-up differs from other types of pick-up (in a bar, for example) in that there is no overt desire to mate. The exception here is pairs of teenage females who sit on the bench waiting for two young men to complete their game of singles, and who giggle more than is normal among people waiting on benches.

Since these young women often wear very short shorts, and cross their legs just as a man is about to serve, resulting in a double fault and possible damage to the genito-urinary tract, the tennis player needs to keep his concentration, wearing blinkers if necessary.

A typical pre-game exchange between male and female goes like this (and explains the dialectical expression "the ball is now in your court"):

"Excuse me, miss, are you waiting for someone?"

"Yes, I am."

The tennis match (1)

"A friend?"

"Yes, a friend. My girl friend."

"Me, too. I'm waiting for a friend I play with all the time. I can't understand why she isn't here. She's never been late before."

"I think my friend must have had a traffic accident. A serious accident. I was just sitting here wondering whether I should go home and phone the hospital emergency."

"The same thought occurred to me. It doesn't seem

The tennis match (2)

65

right to play tennis when my friend may be lying trapped in a car in a ditch somewhere."

"Gawd, no."

"So why don't we have just a short set?"

"Right. Seven-point tie-breaker."

"You're on, gorgeous."

This is social tennis at its most primitive. The players are in fact abusing the game, reducing it to a courtship activity of the same order as the zigzag dance of the stickleback fish, though the stickleback is often

The tennis match (3)

66

better at the net. For serious tennis the player arranges the game beforehand, with someone he knows, and they arrive at the court at approximately the same time, or at different courts if the message was taken by their secretaries.

Tennis being the game of the upwardly mobile, the question sometimes arises: How should you address your executive superior? Letitia Baldridge, author of *The Amy Vanderbilt Complete Book of Etiquette*, says that the young executive can use the boss's first name

The tennis match (4)

on the tennis court, though not back at the office. To this it should be added that a junior staffer playing with the president of the firm should refrain from becoming overly familiar ("Good shot, Bonny Buns!").

Feminist Tennis

> When lovely woman stoops to volley,
> And finds too late she licked the guy,
> What charm can soothe his melancholy,
> Except to honour wave bye-bye?

The tennis match (5)

The pick-up

A question that bothers many a younger woman today is: How aggressive should I be when playing singles against my boy friend? The man I hope to marry and have father my children. Or at least take me to a better-class motel.

Should I clobber him 6-0 and risk his returning my ring? Or is it more discreet for me to lose convincingly, 0-6, even though I know I'll hate myself in the morning?

This quandary is not peculiar to tennis. The same dilemma causes anxiety in girls who shoot pool. The woman must measure the immediate satisfaction of victory, and possibly winning a wager, against her jeopardizing a more permanent relationship with a male whose sense of manhood is directly linked to lording it over the female in any game except rope skipping.

Some men are so wary of losing their bachelorhood that they are ready to suspect their female opponent of deliberately throwing the match. When she serves doubles ten times in a row, the hair rises on the back of his neck. He can practically smell the orange blossoms, hear the organ playing "O, Promise Me."

A woman should therefore go all out to trounce her fiancé, regardless of how much time she has put into making his mother like her.

If her boy friend doesn't have enough emotional security to be able to handle a thrashing by her on the tennis court, she being only five feet tall and weighing 110 pounds, then of what value is his looking like John

Point. . . Set. . . Match. . .

Travolta and having the wealth of an Arab prince? The girl should dump him at once and find an ugly truck driver who thinks a foot fault is fallen arches.

If a woman is really determined to go overboard to win, she may try deck tennis.

However, to compensate for winning set after set over the man in her life, she may also consider knitting him a racket cover. With an appliqué of hearts. The lady should present the racket cover to her lover after she has administered a particularly humiliating defeat, so that he can put the racket cover over his head till well clear of the club.

Possession as Nine-Tenths of the Law

Assuming that you have had a successful rendezvous with your opponent, how do you remind the incumbents on the court that their playing time is up, without using tear gas? It is a good idea to wear a cheap watch to the court, so that you can stare at it pointedly as you wait on the bench, winding it and if necessary holding it to your ear and shaking it.

Even stronger, fetch your tape recorder and turn up the volume on "When I Grow Too Old To Dream."

If the court hogs ignore these hints, it is quite proper to proceed to ploy No. 2, which is to interrupt their game by yelling at them in mid-rally:

"Excuse me, but my watch seems to be fast. Could you tell me the correct time, to the nearest month?"

Latin tennis

If the respondents have the usual tennis manners, they will both reply "No" and continue playing. What do you do now? Regardless of whether the incumbents are bigger and obviously fitter than you are, discretion advises against inciting direct confrontation, as by urinating on their personal effects. The safer procedure is to put on city parks board overalls and tell the rude players that you have come to repaint the lines on the court.

Needless to say, once you have gained possession of the court, you remove your watch and lose all sense of time. When encroaching players ask you your score (a clumsy attempt to establish that your set is liable to end), you have no recollection of having yet played a point.

72

With more and more public and private courts requiring reservations, so that you must start and finish at a specific time, winning becomes less important than holding the court for the full, allotted period. This circumstance is bad for the competitive spirit but does create a useful alibi: "Our hour is up already? I was just getting warmed up."

Courtesy as a Winner

Once you have managed to grab a court, politeness may be used to disable your opponent psychologically. If the court is wet, take the end with the most puddles. Make a production of your having to use the squeegee, while wearing the beatific look of Moses at the parting of the Red Sea.

Or, if the day is fine, preempt the end where you have the sun in your eyes and the wind in your face. Properly executed, choosing the disadvantaged end can be the next best thing to coming onto the court in a wheelchair. So long as your opponent doesn't remember the rule about changing ends after every odd game, he will never recover fully from your being handicapped by the forces of nature. Victory tastes like ashes to him. He may even be reduced to tears, when you come to the net to congratulate him, your sun-blinded eyes staring sightlessly past him as your hand gropes to shake his.

Needless to say, this strategy should be adopted

only if you believe that you have no chance of winning anyway. If you think you have a chance of beating your opponent, it is more courteous to allow him to precede you onto the court, choosing whichever side pleases him. *He* may attempt the martyr bit, ostentatiously putting on sunglasses to examine cracks in his playing surface. Counter by ignoring his antics, as beneath contempt.

Once on the court, how long should you rally? The point here is that *you cannot lose till you start keeping*

Forcing the backhand

score. Your authors therefore favour a very thorough warm-up against an opponent who has beaten you 99 times out of 100. There is always the chance that while rallying he will break his leg, or be carried off by a large bird. Only the painfully obvious tennis player shows eagerness to engage in actual combat. A studied disinterest in starting the set can unsettle your opponent if he is the hyper-competitive type. When at last he shouts "Shall we have a go?" you have the satisfaction of making him personally responsible for the lop-sided score resulting from your having to commence the contest before you were limbered up.

In order to emphasize your distaste for being "hustled" into the game, you do not remove your warm-up jacket or pants till the score is 0-5, love-forty. Only then do you indicate that your body has finally adjusted to the atmospheric conditions and your opponent's peculiar style of play.

While these tactics help to mitigate the sting of defeat, if not to delay it indefinitely, we must ask ourselves: Are they good tennis manners? The answer: Absolutely. Anything that contributes to making your opponent's victory less sweet acts as a preventive against his developing an inflated opinion of his prowess at the game. Tennis needs more humility. Other people's humility.

Double fault

Alibis

ecause tennis is not a team game, and singles is more popular than doubles, the losing player usually has no one to blame but himself. This is clearly intolerable. The player who gracefully accepts full responsibility for his being skunked may think that he is being a good sport but his opponent will suspect that he is some kind of masochist. Word gets around that he plays tennis only while having reupholstery done on his bed of nails.

Much more acceptable, in places like Palm Springs where tennis is a critical part of the life-support system, is the alibi. A really original and imaginative alibi is admired almost as much as winning itself. It provides an outlet for creativity, in people who have no other perceptible talent. But the alibi must have class. A crude alibi is almost as gross as having no alibi at all.

A simple type of alibi is the playing surface. Whether the surface is clay, grass or hard court, the player, at the outset, makes it plain that it is not the surface that he is accustomed to winning on. The pre-game conversation goes something like:

"Good God, we're playing on asphalt."

"Not asphalt actually, old man. It's called Har-Tru—"

The Bus Ride (1)

(2)

(3)

"Of course, of course. Stupid of me to think that we'd be playing on clay. I learned to play tennis in Poona, you see. Lovely red clay of the Indian outback. Little black chaps dash out between games, sweep the canvas tapes, brush your balls, give you a sip of toddy to sluice down the dust . . . "

(The wrong-surface alibi is solidly supported by the fact that professional players who win the French Open

(4)

on the slow clay surface of Roland Garros in Paris rarely
do well on the fast grass of Wimbledon or the hard
courts of indoor tennis. Grand Slam winners like Rod
Laver have shown an adaptability to surface that must
be viewed as regrettable by any connoisseur of tennis
alibis.)

"...The clay makes for a much more heady
game, don't you think? More strategy, what? None

(5)

of that silly serve-and-volley nonsense that the Yanks depend on. Still, beggars can't be choosers. It's your club, and I'm sure they do the best they can with limited resources. You go ahead and serve a few. I'll be right with you as soon as I've put the extra insoles in my shoes to try to protect my feet from blistering on this tarmac . . ."

Needless to say, when the hard-court player finds himself faced with clay, the alibi is reversed: "Hey, man, is this stuff ever *slippery*! I should have worn baseball cleats. I don't know whether to run for the ball or slide into second," etc.

(6)

BANK

84

Does this use of the playing-surface alibi diminish you as a class tennis player? Unfortunately, yes. As a pre-emptive alibi it suffers from the severe limitation of your being able to use it only when playing on an unfamiliar court. Become too dependent on it and you doom yourself to a nomadic existence, a tennis gypsy, drifting from court to court and being expected to read palms.

A superior type of alibi is that pertaining to physical limitations of the loser. But the player must be cautious about overkill. Arriving at the court on crutches does put one's opponent at an initial psychological disadvantage, but his credibility may be strained when you use the crutches only to change ends.

However, the self-evident disability does make the best physical alibi. The Bourbon kings of France were known to have loose bowels. (They would have preferred to keep it a secret, but it leaked out.) As a result, when they played tennis, and were losing a match, they merely had to walk awkwardly around the court in order to taint the win.

Commonly tennis players use their height as an alibi, a rather tired device. Unlike basketball, football and sex, there is no demonstrable advantage to being tall in tennis. To be short with long arms is preferable to being tall with short arms. This is why a chimpanzee can beat a giraffe at tennis nine games out of ten. Despite this a player losing to a taller opponent will all too often interrupt play to comment "It must be a lot easier to get your first serve in when you can reach over the net," or "I don't suppose you've noticed that there's a ground fog rolling in."

Low-grade alibi. In actual fact the height advantage is cancelled out because messages from the brain take longer to reach the feet. Long legs cover more ground but they can't change direction as quickly, with the result that very lanky players spend much of the game imbedded in the fence.

Tennis is in fact a game for small people. Agility is more important than brute strength. The player must have dancer's legs and should be able to bend the knees at short notice. But his general physique is—and here is the problem—that of the bumptious little mesomorph. Football produces gentle giants, hulks so huge that they compensate by doing community welfare work. But we would be confused to see a TV public-service message of Ivan Lendl or Jimmy Connors with his arm around Timmy, the crippled kid. Even the germs would boggle.

Because magnanimity is not built into tennis by the physical requirements of contact sports played by large people, it is doubly important that one's alibis be impeccable. By far the most distinguished physical alibi in tennis is of course *tennis elbow*. Tennis is one of the few games to have a chronically painful joint named after it. Tennis elbow is as prestigious as housemaid's knee is vulgar. It is an absolutely classic alibi in that

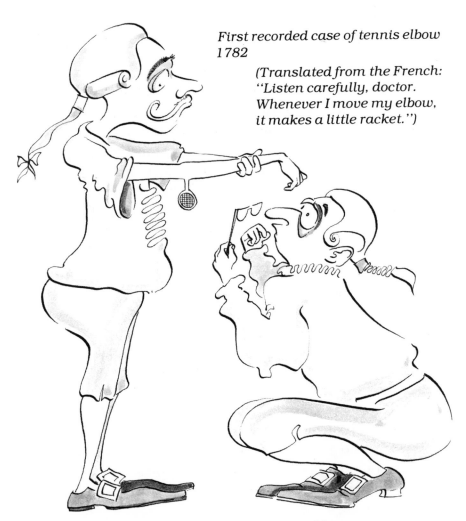

First recorded case of tennis elbow
1782

(Translated from the French:
"Listen carefully, doctor.
Whenever I move my elbow,
it makes a little racket.")

almost nothing can be done for it. Except rest, which the owner of the elbow bravely ignores, along with the excruciating pain, in order to oblige his opponent by playing a game with him.

Tennis elbow is such a popular alibi, however, that the alibi-seeker must familiarize himself with its symptoms and treatment if he hopes to convince an opponent who likely has a tennis elbow of his own, in remission if he's winning but flaring up after the loss of the second set. What, then, *is* tennis elbow? The beauty of the affliction is that anyone can contract it, with unlimited severity. Tennis elbow is a form of bursitis, or inflammation of the bursa. (The bursa has the function of a saloon bar: a fluid-filled space cushioning the joint in use of the elbow. But in tennis you meet a better class of people.)

The inflamed joint is not apparent. That is, it needn't smoke visibly. Or even swell. This makes it ideal for alibiing, since the agony of tennis elbow is well documented without the inconvenience of being demonstrable, as with gout. To draw attention to his tennis elbow, the player usually, before the game starts, ostentatiously pulls an elasticized bandage over the elbow of the arm that wields the racket. If he really doubts his chance of winning a point, he may also wear a bandage on the other elbow, though double tennis elbow is usually confined to switch hitters.

A typical tennis-elbow alibi dialogue goes something like this:

> "Would you mind fastening the pin in this bandage for me? Don't worry about pricking me. I won't even notice, my tennis elbow is that painful."
> "I say, old man, are you sure you should be playing tennis?"

"Oh, yes. Ouch. The doctor says I may as well use the elbow, since it isn't going to get any better."

"Tennis elbow that bad, eh?"

"Terminal, I'm afraid. But don't let it affect your play. It only hurts when I hit the ball . . ."

This is novice use of tennis elbow as an alibi. Rubbery elbow sleeves in gay colours are rampant on tennis courts, simply because increasing numbers of tennis players resort to tennis elbow as their prime excuse for a dismal performance.

The knowledgeable tennis player gets much more mileage out of his tennis elbow. He knows that in last-resort cases the doctor orders injections of cortisone or hydrocortisone. Cortisone treatment can cause sex-change characteristics: women grow hair on their faces, men develop breasts. Do not, therefore, try your tennis-elbow alibi against a male opponent who shows up wearing a training bra, or a female opponent who has to stop and shave between sets. You are up against someone whose tennis-elbow alibi is in the top 100 professional rankings.

Of the other high-profile alibis one of the more visible has been developed by John McEnroe, who frequently enters the championship match wearing a bandage on his thigh. This is the next best thing, visually, to carrying one arm in a sling. The aesthetic effect may be marred, but as a tennis player you must make up your mind: do you just want to look pretty, or will you make the sacrifices required to strengthen an alibi into a world-class excuse?

Remember: alibi preparation is as important as stroke preparation. Essential are good footwork, bending the truth, and following through with a gallant smile despite the hurting. Only the rankest amateur waits till the match is over to show his opponent the blisters on his fingers, or to claw at the alleged gnat in his eye. Belatedly rattling one's wrist to demonstrate the calcium deposits—that is bush. The ruptured Achilles tendon ("The surgeon said I can expect ninety-five-per-cent recovery") seems a splendid alibi, but removing the tennis shoe and sock in order to display the scar makes too much of a good thing, too late.

The tennis alibi, like the quality of mercy, is not strain'd.

This brings us to gross abuse of the alibi, all too common among players of racket games, namely to produce an alibi after you have *won*. Also known as rubbing it in. This utterly contemptible exchange goes as follows:

> *Loser:* Well, Fred, you played a great game. Beat me fair and square.
>
> *Winner:* Certainly a surprise to me. I didn't think I'd be able to make one shot, with my back the way it is.
>
> *Loser:* You have a bad back?
>
> *Winner:* Oh, sure. The old disc problem. Gets me

when I serve. Or bend over to pick up the ball. During the third game of the second set—the game you won—I could hear the old vertebrae going like a xylophone.

Loser (CRYING): I hope I didn't aggravate the disintegration of your spine.

Winner: No problem. My back will never be right, but what the hell—how about another game next week?

Ill-behooving, this. Such cruel and unnatural alibiing can destroy friendships, abort a wedding engagement, and infuse the tennis player with all the charm of a venereal wart.

Tacky Tactics

t is said that Robert Louis Stevenson got the idea for his novel *Dr. Jekyll and Mr. Hyde* while playing tennis. He merely changed the situation of the hero to drinking an evil potion in the lab instead of taking his shots from the baseline.

Be that as it may, tennis does transfigure the player into a kind of zombie, because of *concentration*. Even his orange juice is from concentrate.

Some serious tennis players are so highly concentrated that they don't run at all. They congeal into the service stance, staring at the ball in their hand, and have to be fork-lifted off the court. Those that manage to

95

combine concentration with actual movement of the body commonly develop various stupefying tics, such as bouncing the ball on the court numerous times before serving. To establish his concentration, the server has to bounce the ball exactly the same number of times before both his first and second service. Otherwise his concentration is broken, and nothing on God's earth can repair the broken concentration of a profes-

Show-off tennis
("So I says to Jimmy . . .")

Show-off tennis (Overdoing the pizzaz)

sional tennis player. They may as well bury him where he stands.

Occasionally the concentrating player becomes so fascinated by his preliminary bouncing of the ball that he never gets around to serving. He may be subconsciously hoping that his opponent will become hypnotized, or tire of watching him bounce the ball and after an hour or so will pack up and go home. Winning by default does not faze the serious tennis player. He is happy to shake hands with himself.

Intelligent aggression

The purpose of all this intense concentration is to put the ball where the opponent cannot reach it. This gives the tennis player a wonderful feeling of fulfilment. Only the novice is under the impression that he serves in order to put the ball in play.

When a tennis player casts his bread upon the waters, he tries for an ace.

Despite his concentration, the player often misses with his first serve and must take a second ball (which he has craftily hidden about his person) and try again. Having to resort to a second serve puts him in a foul mood because the ball travels more slowly and his opponent has a better chance of returning the serve, thereby ruining the server's entire day.

Errors in tennis are of two kinds: *forced errors* and *unforced errors*. Your having more *forced* errors than your opponent may help to explain why he beat you. Your having more *unforced* errors means that you have beaten yourself (auto-flagellation). The player who commits too many unforced errors may lapse into a deep depression, digging a hole if he can't find one. For this reason the player who wants to improve his game in terms of mental health must *never admit to himself that any of his errors have been unforced*. The Devil made him do it. For the tennis player who does not believe in the Prince of Darkness and His infernal power to make you miss a sitter, the authors have personally tested the following causes of a tennis error that might otherwise seem unforced:

Show-off (1)

99

(a) The noise of jets taking off. (Less effective if you are playing more than 100 miles from the nearest airport.)

(b) Coming from a broken home.

(c) Chronic anxiety because of the threat of nuclear war.

(d) Mother on cocaine.

Note that these forcements are distinct from alibis, which are voiced to one's opponent before or after the game. These are purely internal factors that make an unforced error inevitable. When we see the tournament pro sitting motionless between games, apparently oblivious of his surroundings, what he is doing is telling himself, "I served those doubles because my parents

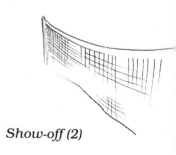

Show-off (2)

started me too early on toilet training." Or "I would not have flubbed that easy volley were I not very concerned about the influence of interest rates on the economy."

Even with a full repertoire of reasons for his unforced errors, a player must, and indeed should, from time to time admit that he has lost a point because of a forced error. That is, his opponent made a lucky shot that proved to be a winner. (A typical forced error is when your opponent, in desperation, makes a drop shot to which you reply by sliding along the court on your chin, at the same time butting the ball firmly into the net.)

Show-off (3)

Too many forced errors can discourage a player unless he sees each for what it is: *a cheap shot.* Notably the chop shot, the hop shot, and the drop shot. An opponent who consistently uses the drop shot to force your errors raises doubts about his manhood. The question is, how do you deal with this kind of hormone-deficient play?

You smile.

As a defensive weapon, the smile is one of the most underrated in tennis. The player can put almost as much twist into his smile as into his serve. When beaten by the effete drop shot, for example, your smile says, in effect: "When are you moving to San Francisco?" Or, "You have certainly been very successful in adapting your strokes to a limp wrist."

This use of the smile applies of course to male players. For a woman, the smile insinuates the opposite, namely that her female opponent's strong winner from the baseline was made possible by her having an abnormal gland producing testosterone. For both men and women, however, the implication of the smile is the same: your opponent won the point at the cost of a normal sex life.

How do you counter your *opponent's* smile? Suppose that you have just won the point by executing a freakish lob off the frame of your racket. The smirk in the opposite court threatens to rob you of the satisfaction of having hit a winner. Do you:

(a) apologize for a fluke?

(b) examine your racket as though the mishit was caused by structural fault?

(c) get off a little joke ("I practise that shot a lot")?

Actually, none of these. Any overt acknowledgment of a weird winner is bad because you may do something equally fortuitous on the next point. The appropriate play here is to act cool, as though your

The Central American Open

Questionable tactics

court strategy is solidly based on dumb luck. (Kissing a rabbit's foot, between points, lends support.) The point is, it will quickly wipe the smile off your opponent's face if he is persuaded that you are fated to win, because you are enchanted.

The serve

(1)　　　(2)

Once he starts to believe that all your net-cord shots are going to fall on his side of the net because it is kismet, his confidence will come apart faster than a five-dollar restring.

To sum up: It is quite possible to play freaky, infuriating tennis without any apparent sign of unpleasantness. This is the seemly way to win, unless of course you are prepared to go to the trouble of learning to play the game properly.

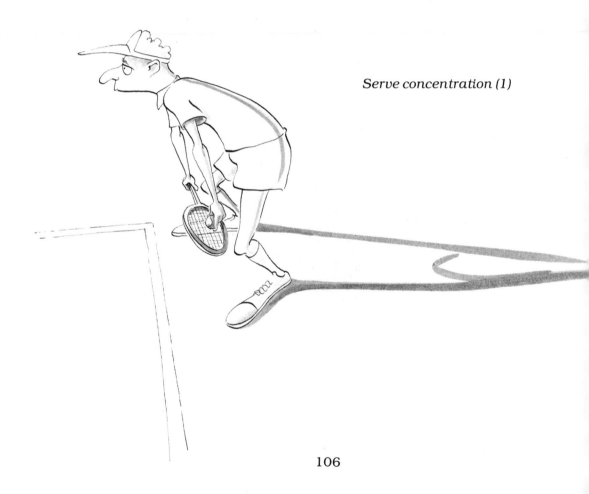

Serve concentration (1)

Serve concentration (2)

Serve concentration (3)

Behaviour modification (1)

(2)

109

Mixed Doubles

Playing mixed doubles presents special opportunities to show no class at all. The male partner, if unseasoned in the hazards of heterosexual relations on the court, is apt to lam the ball directly at the opposing female. Especially if she is his wife. Mixed doubles offers this connubial release of aggression to couples who are willing to break up for the game rather than on other grounds of physical or mental cruelty.

However, picking on the female opponent in mixed doubles is not only boorish but usually counter-productive. For instance, if you volley the ball hard into the lady's stomach, her partner may be enraged

Mixed doubles:
(1) Low-percentage serve

enough to do the same thing to you, rather than to your female partner, resulting in your experiencing more pain than was in your game plan.

Almost as parlous is to serve a cannonball at the opposing male, then let up and serve an exaggerated softie to the woman, to enflame her feminism. Some old fools have even been known to serve underhand to a woman, at the same time hallooing "Here it comes, dear!" Today's woman expects and indeed demands that she be treated like a man. She will be truly flattered if you direct more vicious shots at her than at her male partner, and may even let you win a rally or two as invitation to a more intimate relationship.

This is probably as good a place as any to discuss

Mixed doubles:
(2) Cross court

the role of *sexual distraction* in tennis. The authors, being normal males in most respects, are acutely familiar with this hazard and its potentially devastating effect on one's timing, concentration, and saliva output in a game where spitting is considered to be gauche.

The provocative vista is most prevalent when you are playing in a cluster of courts, side by side and end to end, so that a particularly subversive pair of short shorts keeps intruding upon your field of vision no matter how sedulously you close one eye and squint through the other. In these circumstances the prudent course (wearing blinkers is hell on the peripheral vi-

Mixed doubles:
(3) Excessive backspin

sion) is to manoeuvre your opponent into the end of the court that has the best view of the sex object. Assuming, that is, that your opponent is of the opposite sex to the sex you are opposite. Is this clear?

However, if titillative tennis is what you are into, you may as well enjoy yourself while you lose, love-six. For the male player there is virtually no defence against the mixed-doubles opponent who stations herself at the net and leans forward in a scoop-neck peasant blouse.

Mixed doubles:
(4) Learning process

Presumably the woman player has the same problem playing against the hairy-chested hulk who fills his shorts like Tom Selleck. Tennis has become the most heterosexual game played in public. If you have a low threshold of arousal you should seriously consider taking up some sport that presents less temptation to take your eye off the ball—skydiving, say.

The Tennis Parent

Early conditioning

he big advance of tennis over Gothic types of monster production (such as Dr. Frankenstein's) is that both generations—the tennis parent and the tennis child—develop horrendous features together. As soon as the rich kid shows some skill in handling the racket, his family moves him or her to California or Florida where the prodigy can practise all year 'round. Thus the child has ideal conditions in which to listen to his parents yell at him, day after day. Boys grow up believing that all meaningful communication is made through a wire fence. Girls sometimes develop pelvic stress fractures which later on make it difficult for them to become pregnant unless they have been seeded in a tournament approved by the United States Tennis Association.

What can you do to avoid becoming (a) a tennis parent or (b) a tennis brat? One way is to be poor. Poverty provides 90 per cent protection against conceiving a tennis child. Divest yourself of all your worldly possessions, and the chances are good that your offspring will engage in a sport that suits destitution— mud wrestling, for instance. For 100 per cent protection, however, the potential tennis parent must take a vow of chastity. The actual wording of the vow, as formulated by an order of tennis-playing monks in southern France:

"I swear, by Almighty God, that if tempted to know the flesh of woman or, to be on the safe side, man, I will throw myself into the net, and I will speak to none but the umpire, and I will bite the handle of my racket till I no longer feel the urge to beget a tennis child."

On analysis the vow of chastity is less practical for tennis players who want to have a family. The reproductive urge can be very strong, especially for women, who may be difficult to persuade that they would be better off raising an alligator, or piranha, or some other species that normally gets in a low percentage of first serves.

You are well-to-do, you love playing tennis, and tests indicate the foetus to be not only human but healthy. Is there any merit in pre-natal conditioning of the child to hate tennis? ("My mother was frightened by an angled volley.") Unfortunately this is an old tennis wives' tale. There is no clinical evidence to prove that a tennis player can be nipped in the bud. When the bud has opened into the little stinker: this is the time to take the preventative measures against the malignant growth known as "too much, too soon."

Sometimes it is the mother who takes the initiative.

"There is no such thing as the Bogeyman," she tells her toddler, "but if there were, dear, he would look like your father chasing a lob." This verbal vaccine loses its effectiveness when the child is old enough to discover that the parent he respects is sneaking off to the tennis court, carrying his or her racket in a violin case.

For wealthy parents who holiday in places like the Caribbean it is almost impossible to maintain the illusion that if a person plays tennis his face will break out. Their child meets other children who are well on their way to becoming tennis insufferables, swaggering around in stylish togs and mirrored shades, and carrying multiple rackets, and, presto, he no longer accepts his parents' exhorting him to go hang around a pool hall.

It can be a nasty shock to the parent, the first time he finds a copy of *World Tennis* magazine hidden under a sofa cushion. Already it is too late to buy the kid a Harley-Davidson and leather jacket, and give him the address of the membership secretary for Satan's Angels. When the youngster is repeatedly late for dinner, it is safe to assume that he is banging tennis balls against a backboard somewhere. At this point some parents simply break down, weeping in each other's arms, wondering where they went wrong. Futile self-reproach.

Or, worse, the parents may interpret the child's interest in tennis as merely an alternative lifestyle. They try to look on the bright side of his drinking

Perrier water, instead of beer or bay rum. They introduce him to tennis classes, coaching and, inevitably, the club junior tournament at which the father becomes involved in a punch-up with the opposing father in the stands. The mother makes a needlework plaque for the kitchen that reads WINNING ISN'T EVERYTHING—IT'S THE *ONLY* THING.

Commitment (Doubles)

125

By age twelve the tennis child is committed. There can be no turning back, for him or her, or for the parents. Either the kid is going to become a ranked tennis player, or he will have led a wasted life. He has developed a personality that makes him unsuited for any other career except a Paris waiter.

The tennis parent therefore makes every effort to help the prodigy to develop *the killer instinct*. The killer instinct being essential to winning a major tournament, the parent encourages the child to pull the wings off flies. The son or daughter is coached to take advantage of any weakness. If the opponent is playing on a sprained ankle, run him from sideline to sideline. Wears glasses? Aim the ball at his face.

The tennis mother serves the child's steak raw, and he has to catch it on the first bounce. While she may not commend to her daughter the example of the Amazon women, who cut off one breast to better their pulling the bow, she will repeatedly badmouth Dolly Parton as being physically incapable of hitting a backhand.

Can anything be done to immunize a mother or father against becoming a tennis parent? Aside, that is, from breaking the child's leg? Fortunately, yes. Today special counselling is available to the parent who finds that he or she is unable to stay out of the stands when the offspring is playing. In most large communities the human resources department includes a social worker who specializes in behaviour modification of the tennis parent. The social worker takes the parent to a skid-row bar and keeps him drinking till the kid's match is over. When this program succeeds, the parent has become an alcoholic but he has lost all interest in whether his flesh and blood ever plays at Wimbledon.

If all else fails for you, as a tennis parent, arrange to have your child stolen by gypsies. Relatively few gypsies play tennis. When they lay their hands on some gut, they use it to restring their violins. They may teach your child how to play the fiddle in an ethnic restaurant. You owe it to him.

Geriatric Tennis

Hanging in

They also serve who only stand and wait.

Milton

ou are not getting older,
baby, you are getting bitter. Is this your problem? Do
you gaze at your aging knees and ask "What's a nice
joint like you doing in a game like this?" If so, you are
into geriatric tennis, or the art of growing old disgrace-
fully.

Several factors help to make tennis after forty even
more perverted than in the wormwood-salad days. The
most obvious of these is that the court gets bigger.
Whether or not this phenomenon is related to the theory of an expanding universe, it is demonstrable that
the older player finds himself handicapped by trying to

cover an elasticized court, of which his side stretches intolerably while his opponent's shrinks to a postage stamp.

By sixty, with the natural shortening of the body plus the curvature of the earth, the player experiences the disturbing effect of watching his opponent disappear below the horizon. It is hard to anticipate a ball that seems to reenter the earth's atmosphere without a word from NASA.

However, even under ideal conditions (*i.e.*, when he can see his opponent in the act of hitting the ball back), the older player finds that his body responds more slowly than during the period of his life when his playing time was not dependent on his Duracell battery. Tennis manuals stress the need for preparation, in court coverage—what they call a Tennis Episode. In a typical Tennis Episode, the player:

(a) rises on the balls of his feet, racket high,
(b) rotates the shoulder for racket preparation,
(c) crosses left foot in front of right (unless left-handed),
(d) completes the stroke by returning to the (a) position.

The older player is still rising on the balls of his feet when the ball goes past him. He either performs (b), (c), and (d) as a kind of Chinese exercise (Tai Chi), or he simply subsides back on his heels while snarling "I wasn't ready!"

In order to reach the ball the senior player must start running for it early, preferably the day before the game. This calls for *anticipation*. The older the player, the more exquisite his anticipation must be. This means a long warm-up rally, so that he can learn where his opponent is most likely to place a shot from backhand or forehand. Then, if his opponent insists on

Tennis widow

keeping score, he plays the percentages by running towards a given spot on the court even before his opponent hits the ball. Sometimes he will guess wrong. He goes one way, the ball the other. He should show no remorse. Nor should he attempt to change direction. Instead he slows gradually, pumping the brakes rather than jamming them on, and congratulates his opponent by saying "Damn, but it's hard to judge those mishits."

To try to change direction, for any reason, is the worst mistake an older tennis player can make. Instead of his hearing his racket ping, it's his Achilles tendon. All the hamstrings dry out with age, making them as brittle as cheese sticks. Once he starts tottering forward, therefore, the senior player should continue with his momentum till he collides, gently, with the net, which slingshots him back to his point of departure in plenty of time for tea.

Better yet—if you are over seventy and want to spare yourself six weeks on crutches—don't move your feet at all. Many senior players build their game around the one-shot rally. They depend heavily on their service, to eliminate the need to involve their legs in a suicide mission. Theirs is a game of serve-and-forget-it. Very old tennis players, feigning senility, use a variety of serves to make sure that the ball is not returned. Some serve the second ball before the first one has landed in the opponent's court, then cup their ear and yell "In?" Others put a cut on the ball that makes it hop

Fast return

like a goosed mole. This exasperates the opponent, especially if the balls are his that the miserable old creep is methodically de-fuzzing.

The wily greybeard may also equalize physical condition by causing his opponent to sprain a wrist. He does this by interrupting play to test the height of the net with his racket, meticulously, as though his shots are honed to a thousandth of an inch.

"Ah-ha! As I thought, the net is low. Would you mind adjusting the tension, please? No, up a little. Oops, down a little. Too much. Up a fraction . . ."

Since the crank is a notoriously vicious device, there is an excellent chance that the opponent will have to continue the game with strained ligaments. This is not nice, and even the most venerable of tennis players should use the tactic only if his opponent has a history of beating the crap out of him.

Even more lamentable is the elderly tennis player who does not hesitate to cheat. He has his own ethical code of never calling his opponent's shot out when it is in, unless the point is a crucial one. Then his eyesight fails him. He falls prey to a rare optic condition in which a straight line appears to bend when approached by a round object.

However, when it is the veteran's ball that is called out by his opponent when it lands within a foot of the line, he is thunderstruck. He may not challenge the call overtly, but something in his manner—the dropped jaw, the racket falling from nerveless fingers, the slow walking to the bench to take a tranquilizer pill—indicates his disbelief. His opponent, if younger and with other plans for how he spends the rest of his life, is thus discouraged from making any more close calls. This of course is the purpose of the whole exercise by the crafty oldster, who then merely has to reverse the score a couple of times to win the set.

This style of play is fine, so long as the elderly player is prepared to go to the grave alone and unloved, his passing mourned by none but his chiropractor. But is this enough? Should not the older player provide the younger ones with a model of losing graciously? Of behaving as though there are other things more important in life than thrashing someone 6-0? Certainly. So how does the senior attain this plateau of exemplary sportsmanship?

One way is for the older tennis player to have a

lobotomy. Once the frontal lobes of the brain have been severed, a certain *laissez-aller* attitude characterizes one's game. This rare congeniality in a tennis player may, however, be offset by his losing bladder control. His opponent can be under some pressure to avoid giving him the giggles. The operation is in fact not recommended unless the aging player is already pretty silly anyhow.

The other means of avoiding becoming a dirty old drop-shot artist is to adopt the Hindu or Buddhist faith (if you have not already done so). East Indian tennis players of all ages are invariably courteous and gentle,

because it is against their religion to kill anything, including a short lob. It may take your family a while to get accustomed to the cow wandering unmolested through the house, but down at the tennis club you will be known as "that lovely old soul who smiles and bows when you ace him."

Warning: Playing against an older person may be hazardous to your mental health. As with playing against a member of the opposite sex to whom you wish to be chivalrous, letting up on your game can destroy you. One thing you can be sure of in this world: if you are playing against a seventy-four-year-old grand-mother and you pull your punches, she will eat your ass. Probably in straight sets. Worse, your normal game will be so corrupted by your soft serves and tenderized volleys that it may never recover. You are psyched out for life.

In tennis, to kill with kindness is a form of self-destruction. Regardless of the age, sex, or religion of your opponent, be ruthless. In a nice way, of course.

Tennis Surrogates

Greenpeace tennis

ome people — moral cowards that they are—try to escape being athletic finks by playing games that resemble tennis but don't have the same reputation for churlishness. As part of their effort to become wholesome, tennis players switch to squash. It rarely helps. Squash, racquetball, paddle-ball, ping pong—all these are played in a smallish room specially designed to conceal that the player is a property developer. Or a psychiatrist. Or a radio hotline host. In short, someone in whom the milk of human kindness is 2 per cent evaporated.

Unlike tennis, with its patrician origins, the game

of racquets is believed to have originated in debtor's prison, in eighteenth-century England. It was quickly adopted by the wealthy class, however, and brought to Canada by people who were making a career of declaring personal bankruptcy. It was subsequently picked up by Americans who needed a fast, dangerous, and completely insular game to prepare them for serving five years for embezzlement. Today the squash family of racquets is found in luxury apartment highrises and athletic clubs where people can experience the thrill of being mugged without having to leave the building.

Very confused tennis

Losing grip

Tennis as Beanball

New York (Reuters). "... Ivan Lendl let it be known last week that, hereafter, he won't think twice about whipping a 150-kilometre-an-hour forehand smash at McEnroe's head if his interminable bickering sways an official's call or disrupts Lendl's concentration in future matches." (*The Sun*, Vancouver, B.C., 18 May, 1983)

One of the unspoken rules of gentlemanly, or Victorian, tennis was that one did not deliberately attempt to detach an opponent's head, regardless of provocation. This was especially true if one's opponent was a lady, or a member of the royal family. Occasionally the server in mixed doubles would slam the ball into his partner's backside, at the net, but this was deemed to be an accident unless the partners had been married for longer than six months.

Is deliberate physical assault to be a part of tomorrow's tennis? The last time a net was used in one-on-one mortal combat was in the games of ancient Rome, the gladiator called the retiarius being armed with a net and trident. While it seems unlikely that a tennis gladiator will ever enmesh his opponent in the net in order to finish him off with a spiked racket, today's tennis does increasingly have the potential for violence committed on the person of one's adversary. Could it be that for the Championship, Wimbledon, of June 1995, the commentator (Howard Cosell, Jr.) describes the action . . .

Good afternoon, tennis fans, from this venerable shrine to strawberries and cream, where today on the centre court we are about to witness the finals of the gentlemen's singles. The court is in excellent condition—the attendants have raked sand over the places made slippery with blood after yesterday's semi-final match between Ivan the Barbarian and The Texas Terror. Ivan's body is already on its way back to Czechoslovakia, where he will be buried in an unmarked grave with his favourite racket.

Today The Texas Terror meets the other finalist, the unseeded young African sensation, Bush Bongo. Bongo's unique style of tennis, in particular his crushing backhand for which he uses both hands and one foot, has persuaded the umpire to turn thumbs down on several of Bush

Canadian tennis

Bongo's opponents whose lives might otherwise have been spared.

Ah, but I see that the players have completed their warm-up and removed their flak jackets. The Texas Terror is naked but for the stainless steel athletic cup that stood him in good stead against the wicked forehand of the Barbarian, who made the mistake of sacrificing mobility to armour and was felled by a volley straight into his beaver.

Bush Bongo serving . . . a cannonball aimed

at the body! The Terror did well to sidestep the celebrated "widowmaker," which has been clocked at 200 kilometres an hour. Bush Bongo never tries to get his first serve into the court. His object is to make a clean, round hole through his opponent's midsection, then exploit that advantage for the remainder of the match. . . .

Bongo's second serve is very, very high. Another of his feared tactics: while his opponent is gazing skyward, waiting for the ball to come down, Bongo hurls his racket—yes, there it goes!—like a boomerang at the head of The Texas Terror. But the Terror anticipates beautifully, ducks the razor-sharp frame of the whirling projectile, and hits the serve back for a winner into Bongo's left ear. That polite applause from the crowd indicates that Bush Bongo is the sentimental favourite here at Wimbledon, particularly since he lost his nose in the third round. . .

If tennis is to be spared this fate (an extension of all-out karate), those of us who enjoy it as a friendly game are duty bound to resist its brutalization. One way to cushion the confrontation is to add more *humour* to tennis. At the moment tennis is the most sourpuss of spectator sports. There is no such thing as a tennis joke, with the possible exception of Bobby Riggs. Old tennis buffs do not gather around the hot stove to exchange amusing yarns, because hardly ever does a funny thing happen on the way to the forecourt. Professional tennis is leavened by nothing like the San Diego chicken.

What tennis needs from the media is less attention to the cry-baby antics of the players whose spiritual growth has been stunted by pernicious narcissism. Let's hear more of the human-interest story . . .

Wimbledon. The tennis world today mourns the retirement of Sir Geoffrey Hoodspith-Bullminster, senior net judge. At the age of eighty-seven, Sir Geoffrey has called more "Lets!" than a nymphomaniac. Today he steps down, or rather stands up, voluntarily. "I simply don't trust my judgment any more," he told a press conference of tennis writers. "I don't have it in the finger any more. The sensitivity, you know. My wife noticed it first. She told me: 'Geoffrey, darling, in your prime you could detect the slightest quiver of the net cord. It was what drew me to you. That and the natural elegance with which you straddled

1. Baseline error

the post. Now, the ball can hit the tape with an audible whack, jump high into the air and bounce off your head, but it merely wakes you up to say "Time for tiffin, dear?"'"

For his many years of devotion to the service, Sir Geoffrey not only has been knighted but will receive a comfortable pension and the honour of enshrinement, in the International Tennis Hall of Fame, of a plaster cast of his forefinger.

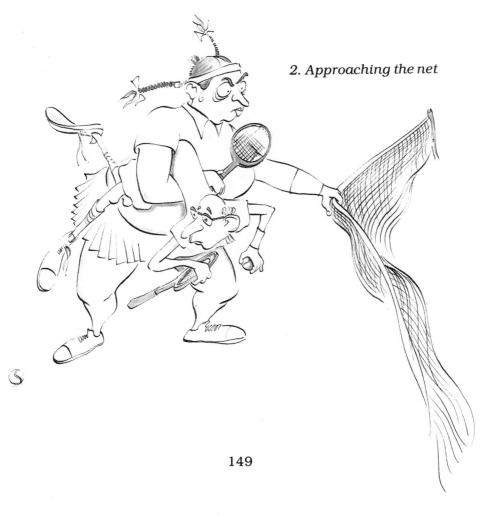

2. Approaching the net

3. Controlling momentum

4. Follow-through

Dear Doctor Tennis . . .

"Rule Number One: Don't overdo."

he following are letters received by the authors from troubled tennis players too ashamed of their affliction to discuss it personally at a tennis clinic. From Ashley Fortescue II (aged seven) of Palm Beach, Florida:

Q: *My Daddy said No when I asked him to act as ball boy. When I asked him then what should I do with the second ball, while I am serving the first ball, he told me where I could put it. But when I put it there it makes me walk funny. Also in the junior tournament I got fined $500 for visible obscenity. Please explain.*

A: At one time it was a sign of manhood to hold three balls in one hand when serving. This practice was discontinued because when a player held up the three balls, to show his opponent that he had them, he looked like a pawnbroker's. Since this was damaging to the image of tennis as a snob game, players went back to holding only two balls and finally only one ball at a time. Hence the quandary: where to stow the second-serve ball?

The ball must be retrieved quickly, and without appearing to feel yourself up. This can be achieved by holding the supplementary ball in your mouth. You may notice some distortion of your cheek, but this will come in handy if you decide to take up baseball, or the trumpet.

Some players simply put the second ball in their shorts pocket. This makes an unsightly bulge, however, especially on women who are already a bit hippy. But it is probably a safer repository than carrying the ball in a ventral pouch (Australian mode) or in a sporran (Royal Scots Tennis, Croquet and Usquebaugh Club).

Q: *How big can a racket head be and still remain legal?* (Flo La Rue, Las Vegas Sporting House, Nevada)

A: Any racket is legal in Nevada.

The main problem is that people may think you bought a racket with a big head to match your own. You may hear remarks such as "I'd like to borrow your big-head racket, but I hate to break up a set."

Q: *I have played tennis enough many years to have seen white balls, yellow balls, and green balls. My eyesight is no hell, at seventy, and last week in a seniors' tournament I found myself serving a ball with "Sunkist" on it. It didn't bounce worth a damn. What I want to know is, what is the proper, dignified, official colour for tennis balls? Or should I just dye my own balls, and go for polka dots?* ("All Balled Up," Toronto, Ont.)

A: You old fool, what a dumb question! Seasoned tennis players know that the state-of-the-art tennis

ball is the new Chameleon, by Slazenlop. This ball changes colour to blend with your background, making it very difficult for your opponent to see it unless he wears special glasses. Needless to say, you shouldn't open your can of Chameleon balls till you have exhausted all other means of winning the game unfairly.

To sum up: Tennis can be a beautiful game, played by charming people. It hasn't happened recently, but the potential is there.

If you, dear reader, having read the chapters preceding, are still in doubt about your ability to play the game without giving up your membership in common humanity, we recommend that you see a psychiatrist. The chances are that the psychiatrist plays tennis. You should feel under the couch, when he isn't looking, in case he has hidden his racket there. Definitely avoid the analyst who interviews you while wearing his tennis shorts and a headband that says YAMAHA. (Unless, of course, he is a Japanese shrink, who may just be going through an identity crisis.)

With the proper balance between competitive spirit and sportsmanship, supplemented with surgical removal of the adrenal gland, there is no reason why your tennis should not have the same positive social connotation as that reflected in the phrase "It's not cricket." One day, with your help, people will describe an unfair, miserable and mean-minded act by saying "It's not tennis."

Meantime, practise your ice skating, because Hell will have frozen over.

The authors, Dave More and Eric Nicol, are the only tennis players ever asked to leave a public-park court because their play was causing Leaf Blight.

Dave More first picked up a tennis racket in a part of the Alberta foothills where the only thing strung up is a horse thief. As for Eric Nicol, he used a tennis ball to play street hockey, till he was 35, and still thinks he has scored at tennis when he puts the ball into the net.

For both players this book has been a labour of love-six, though each demanded his own towel and Carling Bassett's phone number.

This book was designed by David Shaw
Edited by José Druker
Composed by Attic Typesetting Inc.
The photograph above was taken by Yvette Brideau & Blair Pinder
Manufactured by T.H. Best Printing Company Ltd.